Dealing with Addition

Lynette Long, Ph.D.

 Charlesbridge

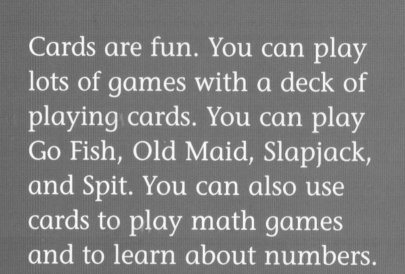

Cards are fun. You can play lots of games with a deck of playing cards. You can play Go Fish, Old Maid, Slapjack, and Spit. You can also use cards to play math games and to learn about numbers.

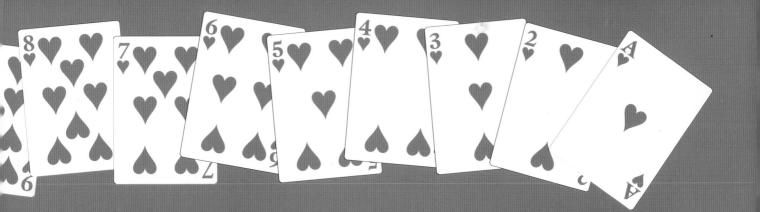

In some card games, you need to match pairs of cards. In others, you need to put cards into groups. Sometimes you need to add the numbers on cards together to find their total. At the end of this book you'll find a game that uses all of these skills!

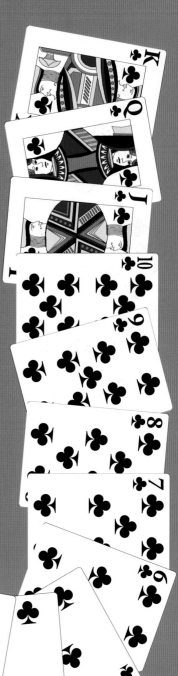

There are 52 cards in a deck. No two cards are exactly alike. Each card has one of four different symbols, or suits, on it:

DIAMOND ♦   SPADE ♠

HEART ♥   CLUB ♣

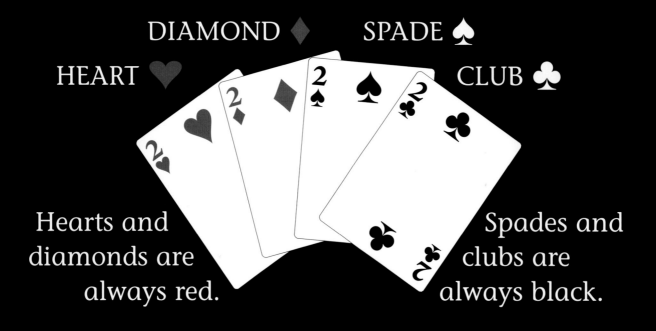

Hearts and diamonds are always red.

Spades and clubs are always black.

Most playing cards have numbers on them. The numbers match the number of big hearts, diamonds, spades, or clubs in the middle of each card.

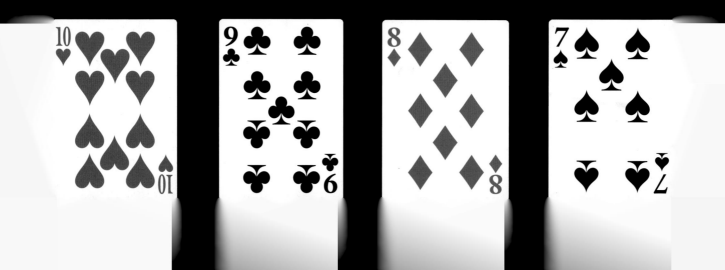

There are no cards with the number one. Cards with only one big heart, diamond, spade, or club are marked with an "A," which stands for "ace." In most card games, each ace acts like the number one.

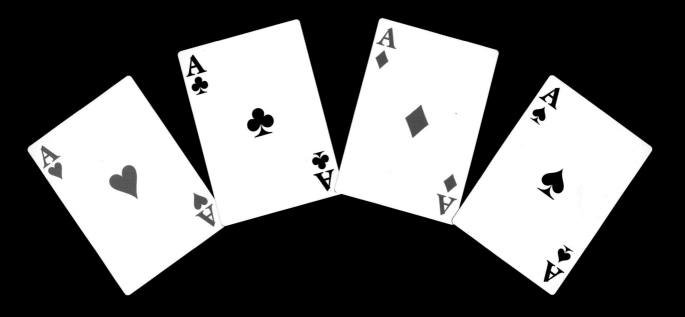

Some cards have a picture of a King, a Queen, or a Jack. Cards with pictures on them are called face cards.

Queen

King   Jack

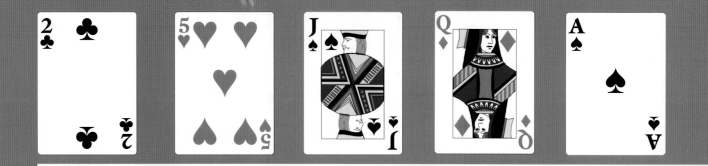

You can put cards together in many different ways. Pick all the red cards from the top of these pages and put them in one group. Put all the black cards in another group.

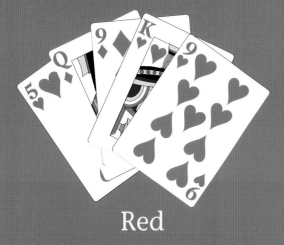

Red

Black

Now put all the face cards in one group and all the number cards in another group.

Face

Number

You can also put cards together by their suits. All the hearts can go in one group and all the diamonds in another group.

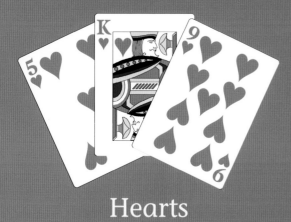

Hearts

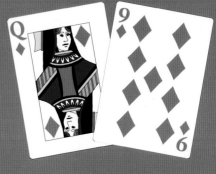

Diamonds

And you can match pairs of cards. How many pairs can you make?

Fives   Twos   Nines

In some card games, you need to find the total of two or more cards. There are two different ways to do this. Some players like to count the big symbols on each card. Others like to add the numbers in the corner of each card. Either way, you get the same answer.

What is the total number of big hearts on these two cards? Find out by counting the hearts in the middle of both cards . . .

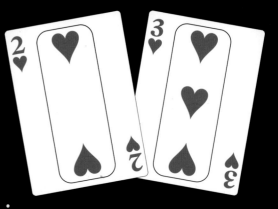

. . . or by adding the numbers in the corners.

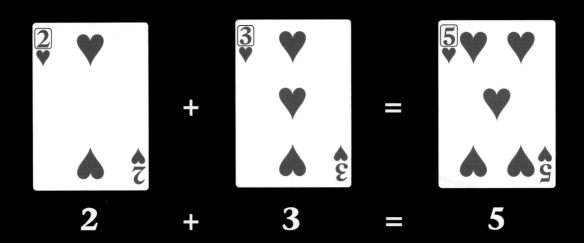

2 + 3 = 5

The total is always five.

You can use addition to find the total of any group of cards. First, add the numbers in the corners to get the total.

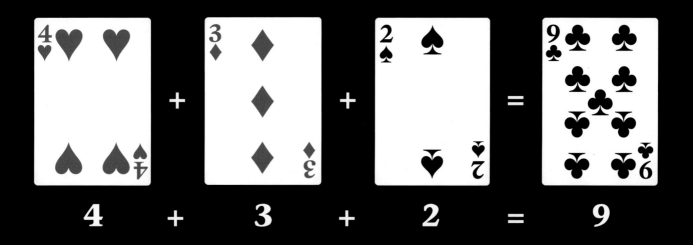

4 + 3 + 2 = ?

Then, count the big symbols. Whether you add or count, the total of these cards is always nine.

If you use cards from different suits, you will get the same total.

4 + 3 + 2 = 9

There are lots of different groups, or combinations, of cards that add up to the same number. Use the cards below and pick all the different ways to get a total of FIVE.

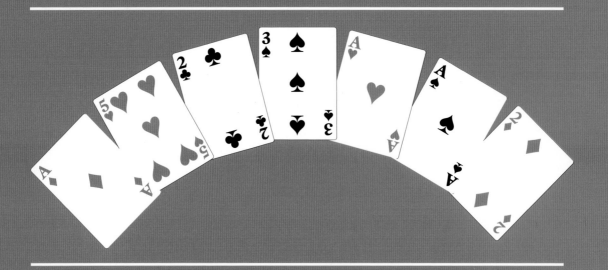

You can pick just the five of hearts. This card by itself gives you a total of five.

5

Or you can put together a three and a two. Either of the twos will work.

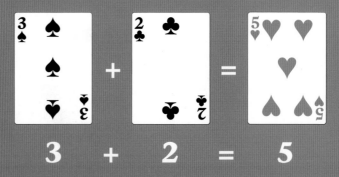

3 + 2 = 5

You can also pick both of the twos
and any ace.

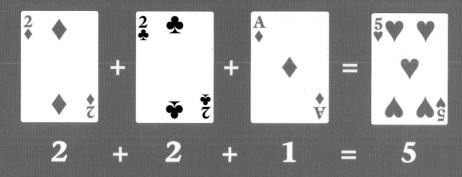

2 + 2 + 1 = 5

You can use a three and any two aces.

3 + 1 + 1 = 5

Or you can pick a two and all three aces.

2 + 1 + 1 + 1 = 5

All of these combinations give you a
total of FIVE.

ONE

You need just one card to get a total of ONE using a deck of playing cards. There are four different aces, one from each suit. Pick any of them and you have a total of ONE.

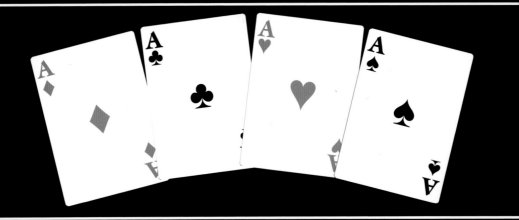

Count the symbol in the middle of this card to be sure. There is just one big diamond.

1

Keep going and find out how to use playing cards to make the numbers up to TEN!

TWO

There are two different ways to get TWO using the cards on this page. Can you pick them out?

First, choose the card or cards that give you a total of TWO. Then, check your work by counting the big symbols in the middle of the cards you have picked.

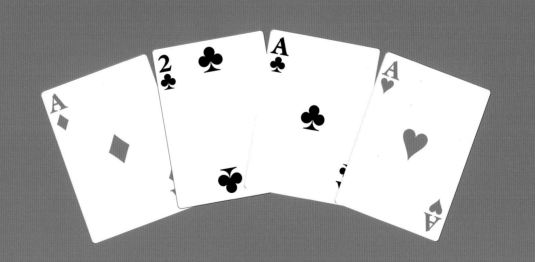

Here are two different ways to get TWO.

2

1 + 1 = 2

You could use any pair of aces and your
addition problem would be the same.

THREE

If you had these cards in your hand, you could find three different ways to get a total of THREE. What are they?

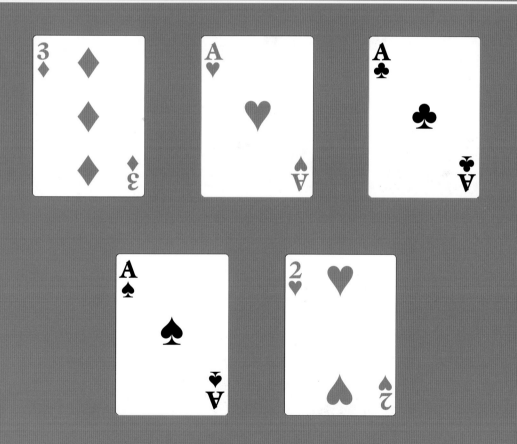

Here are three different ways to get THREE.

3

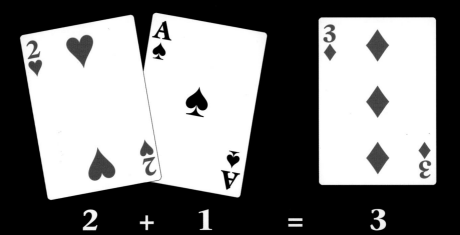

2 + 1 = 3

You could use the ace from any suit and the problem would be the same.

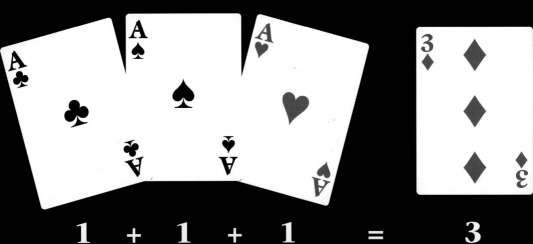

1 + 1 + 1 = 3

FOUR

The larger the total, the more ways there are to get it. The cards on this page give you four different ways to get a total of FOUR. Can you name them?

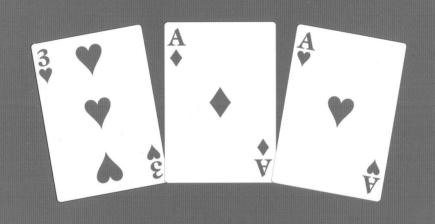

Here are four different ways to get FOUR.

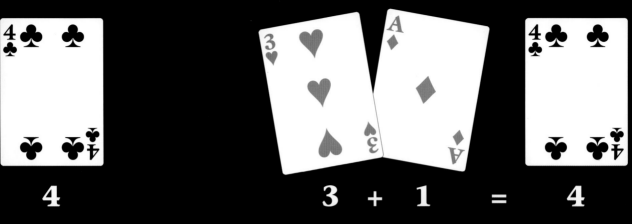

4   3   +   1   =   4

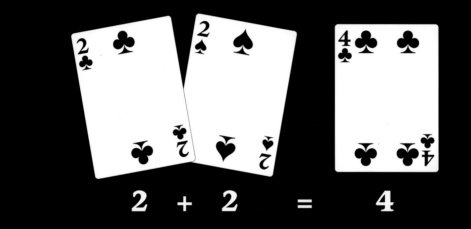

2   +   2   =   4

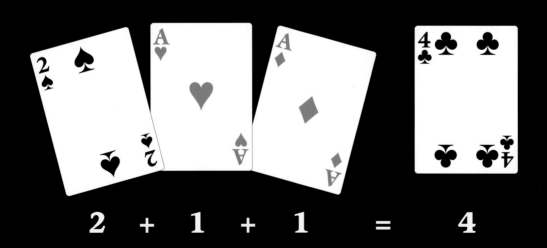

2   +   1   +   1   =   4

Remember, for each total you can use cards
from different suits to make the same problems.

FIVE

You can find five different ways to get a total of FIVE with these cards. Point to each of them.

Here are five different ways to get FIVE.

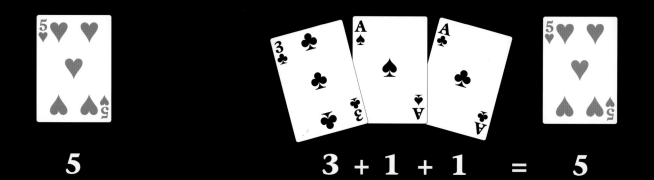

5

3 + 1 + 1 = 5

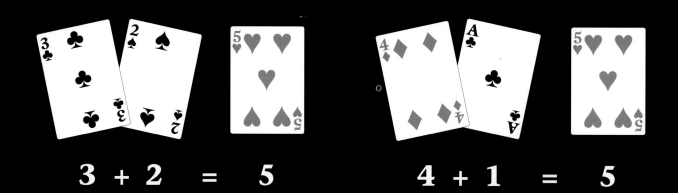

3 + 2 = 5

4 + 1 = 5

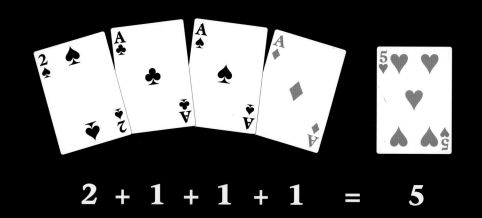

2 + 1 + 1 + 1 = 5

SIX

If you had these cards, you could find six different ways to make SIX. What are they?

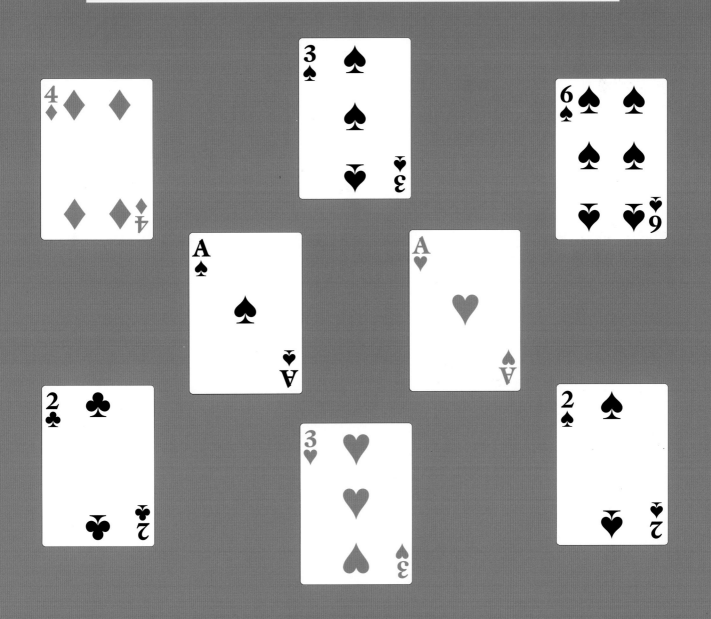

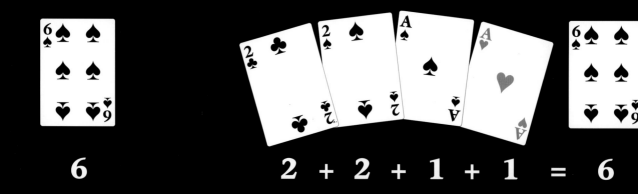

6

2 + 2 + 1 + 1 = 6

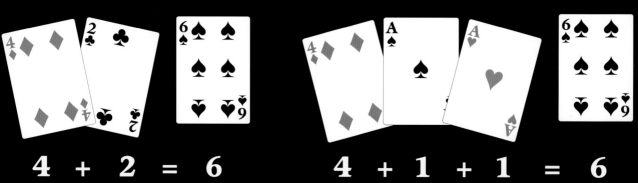

4 + 2 = 6

4 + 1 + 1 = 6

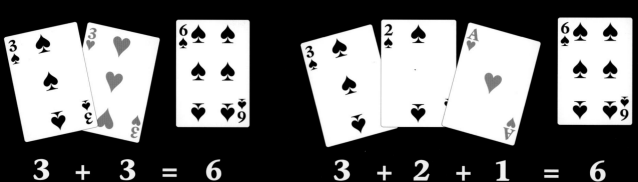

3 + 3 = 6

3 + 2 + 1 = 6

SEVEN

With these cards there are seven different ways to get a total of SEVEN. Can you name all of them?

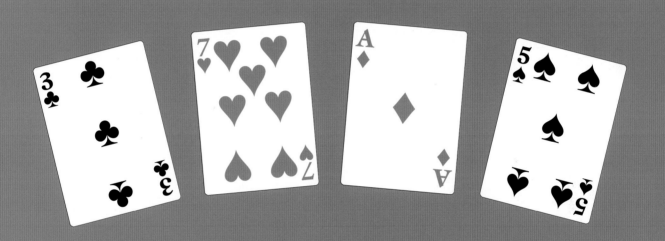

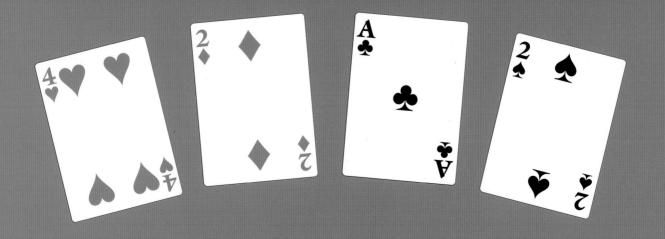

Here are seven different ways to get SEVEN.

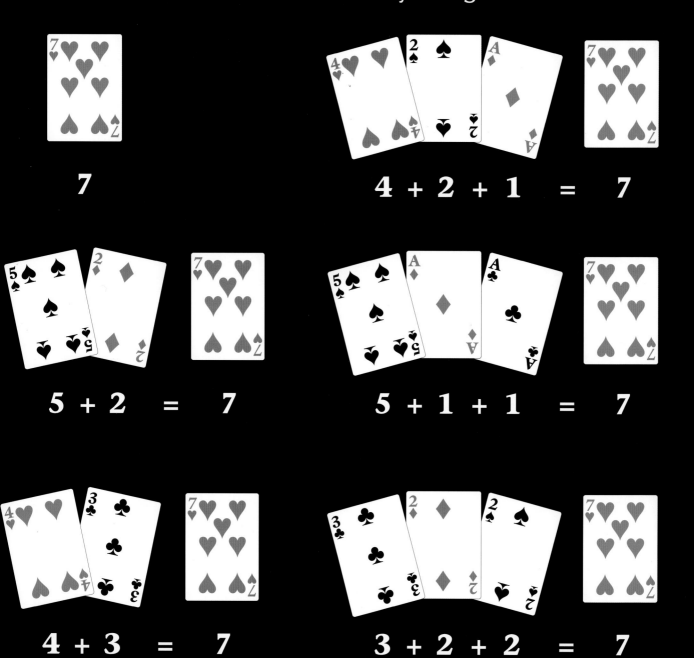

7

4 + 2 + 1 = 7

5 + 2 = 7

5 + 1 + 1 = 7

4 + 3 = 7

3 + 2 + 2 = 7

EIGHT

There are eight different ways to get EIGHT with these cards. Pick out all eight of them.

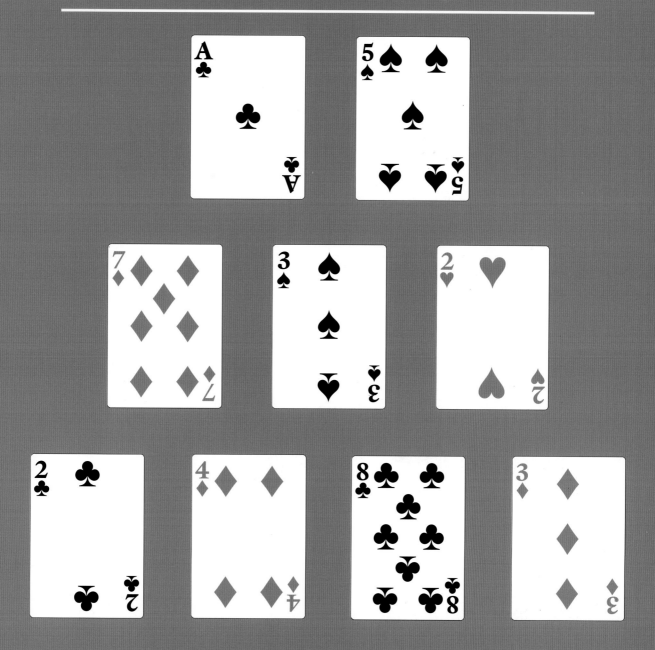

Here are eight different ways to get EIGHT.

8

3 + 2 + 2 + 1 = 8

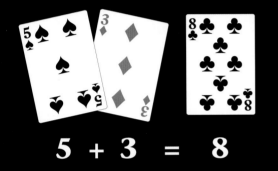

5 + 3 = 8

4 + 3 + 1 = 8

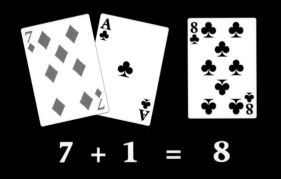

7 + 1 = 8

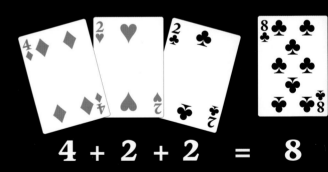

4 + 2 + 2 = 8

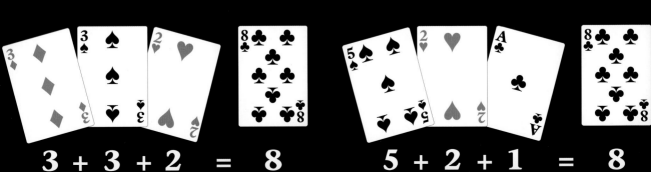

3 + 3 + 2 = 8

5 + 2 + 1 = 8

NINE

Nine different ways to get a total of NINE
can be found on this page. What are they?

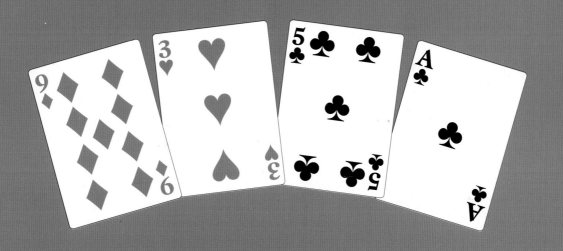

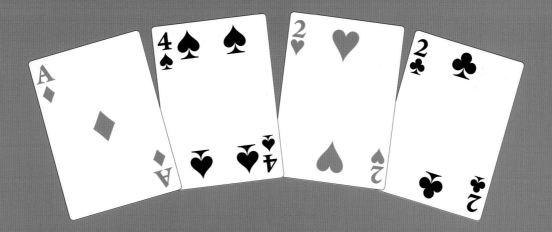

Here are nine different ways to get NINE.

9

5 + 2 + 1 + 1 = 9

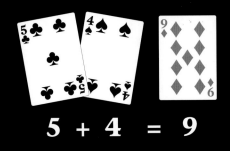

5 + 4 = 9

4 + 3 + 1 + 1 = 9

5 + 3 + 1 = 9

5 + 2 + 2 = 9

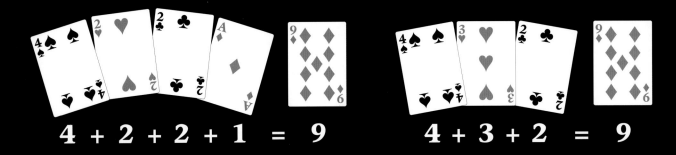

4 + 2 + 2 + 1 = 9

4 + 3 + 2 = 9

3 + 2 + 2 + 1 + 1 = 9

TEN

With these cards there are ten different ways to make TEN. Can you find all of them?

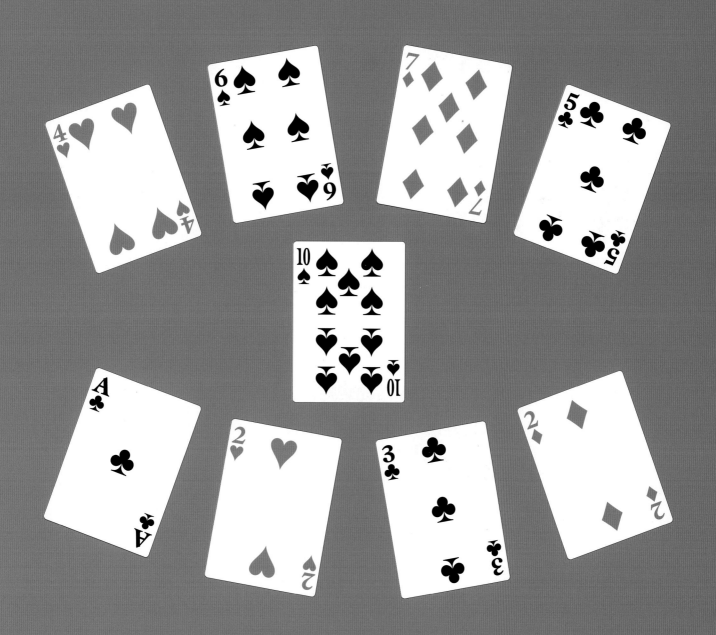

Here are ten different ways to get TEN.

10

5 + 2 + 2 + 1 = 10

7 + 3 = 10

4 + 3 + 2 + 1 = 10

6 + 4 = 10

7 + 2 + 1 = 10

6 + 3 + 1 = 10

6 + 2 + 2 = 10

5 + 4 + 1 = 10

5 + 3 + 2 = 10

Dealing with Addition: The Card Game

Players: Two

Cards: Standard deck of cards with all face cards removed.

Objective: To capture the most cards.

Dealing: The dealer deals four cards facedown to each player and places four cards faceup in a row on the table. During the game, whenever either player runs out of cards, two more cards from the deck are dealt to each player. If the center row runs out of cards, two cards from the deck are placed faceup to make a new row.

Play: The nondealer goes first. Each player tries to match the value of a card or cards in his or her hand to the value of a card or cards in the center row. When a player cannot capture any cards, he or she must lay a card from his or her hand in the center. There are three ways a player may capture cards:

A *pair* is the easiest way to take a card. Make a pair by matching a card in your hand to a card on the table. If you have a 4 of hearts and there is a 4 of clubs in the center, take both cards and put them facedown to the side.

A *table combination* is made by finding two or more cards on the table that add up to the value of one card in your hand. If there are two 4s in the center and you have an 8 in your hand, you win all three cards. Add them to the stack of cards you have captured.

A *hand combination* is won by finding two or more cards in your hand that add up to the value of one card on the table. If you have a 2, a 3, and a 4 in your hand and there is a 9 in the row on the table, you win all four cards. Put them in your stack.

Strategy: Try to take as many cards in each turn as possible. It is always better to take a combination than a pair.

Scoring: The winner is the player with the most cards in his or her stack when neither player can play another card. Cards left in either player's hand or in the center row are not counted in the scoring.

Here are all the ways to make the totals from one to ten with the number cards. Use these combinations when you play "Dealing with Addition."

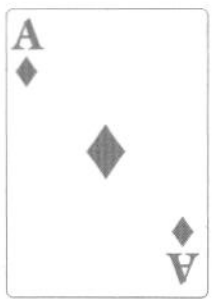

Card					
A	1				
2	2 1+1				
3	3 2+1 1+1+1				
4	4 3+1 2+2 2+1+1 1+1+1+1				
5	5 4+1 3+2 3+1+1 2+2+1 2+1+1+1				
6	6 5+1 4+2 4+1+1 3+3	3+2+1 3+1+1+1 2+2+2 2+2+1+1 2+1+1+1+1			
7	7 6+1 5+2 5+1+1 4+3	4+2+1 4+1+1+1 3+3+1 3+2+2	3+2+1+1 3+1+1+1+1 2+2+2+1 2+2+1+1+1		
8	8 7+1 6+2 5+3 5+2+1	5+1+1+1 4+4 4+3+1 4+2+2 4+2+1+1	4+1+1+1+1 3+3+2 3+3+1+1 3+2+2+1	3+2+1+1+1 2+2+2+2 2+2+2+1+1 2+2+1+1+1+1	
9	9 8+1 7+2 7+1+1 6+3	6+2+1 6+1+1+1 5+4 5+3+1 5+2+2	5+2+1+1 5+1+1+1+1 4+4+1 4+3+1+1 4+3+2	4+2+2+1 4+2+1+1+1 3+3+3 3+3+2+1 3+3+1+1+1	3+2+2+2 3+2+2+1+1 3+2+1+1+1+1 2+2+2+2+1 2+2+2+1+1+1
10	10 9+1 8+2 8+1+1 7+3 7+2+1	7+1+1+1 6+4 6+3+1 6+2+2 6+2+1+1 6+1+1+1+1	5+5 5+4+1 5+3+2 5+3+1+1 5+2+2+1 5+2+1+1+1	4+4+2 4+4+1+1 4+3+3 4+3+2+1 4+3+1+1+1 4+2+2+1+1 4+2+1+1+1+1	3+3+3+1 3+3+2+1+1 3+3+1+1+1+1 3+2+2+2+1 3+2+2+1+1+1 2+2+2+2+1+1 2+2+2+1+1+1+1

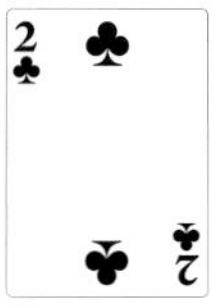

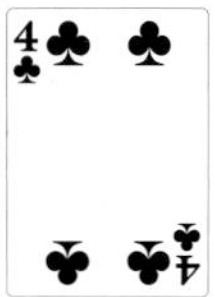

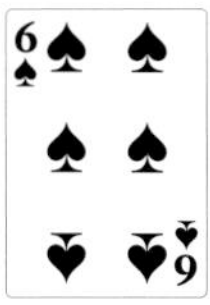

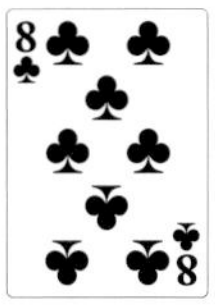

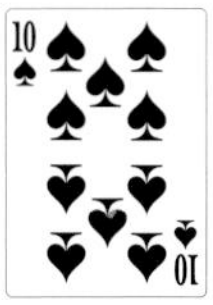

4 ♥ ♥

*To my children,
Seth and Sarah,
the smile in my life
—L. L.*

Published by Charlesbridge
85 Main Street, Watertown, MA 02472
(617) 926-0329
www.charlesbridge.com

Library of Congress Cataloging-in-Publication Data
Long, Lynette.
Dealing with addition/Lynette Long.
p. cm.
Summary: Describes how playing cards can be used to teach addition.
ISBN 0-88106-269-3 (reinforced for library use)
ISBN 0-88106-270-7 (softcover)
1. Addition—Juvenile literature. 2. Playing cards—Juvenile literature.
[1. Addition. 2. Playing cards.] I. Title.
QA115.L717 1998
513.2'11—dc21   97-14075

Printed in Korea
(hc) 10 9 8 7 6 5 4 3 2
(sc) 10 9 8 7 6 5 4 3

The illustrations in this book were done in Adobe Illustrator
and were based on images copyright © 1995 by SoftKey International Inc.
The display type and text type were set in Stone Informal.
Printed and bound by Sung In Printing, Korea
Production supervision by Brian G. Walker
Designed by Diane M. Earley

Other card games that use
addition include:

Blackjack or *Twenty-One*
Casino
Pyramid
Twenty-Nine

♠ ♠ 4 ♠